The Mystery
of the
Bermuda Triangle

Chris Oxlade

Heinemann Library
Chicago, Illinois

Customer Service 888-454-2279

Visit our website at www.heinemannlibrary.com

Designed by **AMR**
Illustrations by Art Construction and Margaret Payne at AMR
Printed in Hong Kong

04 03 02
10 9 8 7 6 5 4

Library Cataloging in Publication Data
Oxlade, Chris
    The mystery of the Bermuda Triangle / Chris Oxlade.
      p. cm. – (Can science solve?)
    Includes bibliographical references and index.
    Summary: Discusses the Bermuda Triangle, an area of the Atlantic
Ocean where numerous ships and airplanes have mysteriously
disappeared, and examines various efforts to identify this phenomena
and discover its causes.
    ISBN 1-57572-811-7 (lib. bdg.)
    1. Bermuda Triangle Juvenile literature. [1. Bermuda Triangle.]
    I. Title. II. Series.
    G558.095 1999
    001.94—dc21   99-18042
                                              CIP

Acknowledgments
The publishers would like to thank the following for permission to reproduce
photographs:

Austin J. Brown, pp. 11, 13, 15; Travel Photography/James Davis, p. 28; Picture
Library/Mary Evans, pp. 5, 6, 9; Eye Ubiquitous, p. 16; S. Lindridge, p. 22; FLPA: D.
Fleetham/Silvestris, p. 7 (inset); H. Hoflinger, p. 17; D. Kinzler, p. 18; Fortean Picture
Library, pp. 24, 27; W. Donato, p. 21; National Archives, pp. 8, 10; The People, p.
29; Trip/E. Smith, p. 7 (main).

Cover photograph reproduced with permission of FLPA/H. Hoflinger.

Every effort has been made to contact copyright holders of any material
reproduced in this book. Any omissions will be rectified in subsequent printings
if notice is given to the publisher.

Some words are shown in bold, **like this.** You can find
out what they mean by looking in the glossary.

Contents

Unsolved Mysteries

For centuries, people have been puzzled and fascinated by mysterious places, creatures, and events. What secrets are held by a **black hole?** Are some houses really haunted by ghosts? Does the Abominable Snowman exist? Why have ships and planes vanished without a trace when crossing the Bermuda Triangle?

These mysteries have puzzled scientists who have spent years trying to find the answers. But just how far can science go? Can science explain the seemingly unexplainable, or are there mysteries that science simply cannot solve? Read on and decide for yourself.

This book tells about the Bermuda Triangle. It looks in detail at unexplained disappearances. It retells eyewitness accounts. It asks if science can account for these bizarre events.

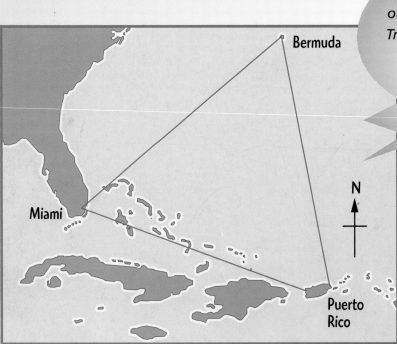

The imaginary outline of the Bermuda Triangle is drawn over a map of the western Atlantic Ocean.

Bermuda Triangle briefing

Bermuda is made up of about 150 small islands, 621 miles (1,000 kilometers) out into the Atlantic Ocean from the eastern coast of the United States. The area known as the Bermuda Triangle is a triangle with its three points in Bermuda; Miami, Florida; and Puerto Rico. The term *Bermuda Triangle* was first used by American journalist Vincent Gaddis in 1964. He wrote a magazine article titled "The Deadly Bermuda Triangle" in which he listed mysterious disappearances in the area.

In the last 200 years, thousands of boats, ships, and aircraft have come to grief in the Bermuda Triangle. Most of these cases have a perfectly reasonable explanation, but almost one hundred of them remain a mystery. Could they be caused by some strange, unknown force? Can science solve this mystery?

JUNE
25 CENTS
IN CANADA 30 CENTS

AMAZING STORIES

Scientifiction Stories by
A. Hyatt Verrill
John W. Campbell, Jr.
Edmond Hamilton

Disappearances in the Bermuda Triangle inspired many wild and wonderful stories in science fiction magazines.

Triangle or trapezium?

Many writers do not agree on the boundaries of the Bermuda Triangle. A few say it is a triangle. Others say it is an elongated shape called the "Devil's Triangle" or "Limbo of the Lost" that stretches further out into the Atlantic Ocean.

Beginnings of a Mystery

It was not until the 1960s that the Bermuda Triangle became famous. But long before that, it was an area of mystery for sailors. The mystery began when early transatlantic voyagers, including Christopher Columbus, first sailed through the Bermuda Triangle area in 1492. They reported unfamiliar sights and strange events.

Christopher Columbus sailed through the Bermuda Triangle on the Santa Maria, *a small ship called a* caravel.

A sea of weed

One of these unfamiliar sights was the area now known as the Sargasso Sea. The sea is an oval-shaped patch of the North Atlantic Ocean. It is several thousand miles across and stretches well into the Bermuda Triangle. The water is usually calm in the Sargasso Sea. It has little wind or **current**. The water is also saltier than the surrounding sea, with very little **plankton** and very few fish. Strangest of all are the great floating masses of seaweed called Sargassum weed. Seaweed is hardly ever found in the open ocean.

This picture shows drifting Sargassum weed being eaten by a Sargassum fish. The weed drifts because the Sargasso Sea has calm waters.

To early sailors, seaweed and the appearance of birds suggested that they were near land, so they were confused when no land appeared. When the weed became tangled with their ships, it slowed them down. The light winds often left them drifting for days on end. It's no wonder, then, that there were tales of ships trapped forever or pulled under the sea by the weeds. Stories spread of sailors being eaten by hideous sea creatures.

During Columbus's first voyage to the area, he reported seeing the lights of a large meteor in the sky. He also noted in his ship's log that the compass pointed to something other than true north. On a return trip ten years later, he lost twelve ships in a fierce **hurricane**. The island of Bermuda was not settled until about one hundred years after that, mainly because it had a reputation as a "place for devils."

No doubt hundreds of ships were lost in the Bermuda Triangle during the following centuries. Many ships, gone without a trace, were assumed to have been sunk by storms. The first ship mentioned in literature about the Bermuda Triangle is the American warship USS *Pickering*. It disappeared without a trace in 1800.

7

Ships and Boats

Losses of ships and boats in the Bermuda Triangle fall in two groups—those in which the ship or boat disappeared without a trace and those in which the ship or boat was found, but the crew was missing.

Spray

The *Spray,* a **sloop** that vanished in 1909, was sailed by Joshua Slocum. He was an experienced sailor and the first man to sail alone around the world. The *Spray* disappeared with the 65-year-old Slocum after he stopped in Miami for supplies.

The disappearance of the Cyclops was described as "one of the most baffling mysteries in the annals of the Navy."

Cyclops

The *Cyclops*, a U.S. Navy **collier**, vanished in 1918. It was 541 feet (165 meters) long, weighed 17,500 tons, and had a crew of 300. It is one of the largest ships ever lost in the Triangle. The *Cyclops* disappeared without a trace while carrying ore from Barbados to the eastern United States. The *Cyclops* was the first ship with a radio to disappear, but the crew sent no emergency message.

Carroll A. Deering

The *Carroll A. Deering,* a five-masted **schooner**, was found abandoned in 1921. It had left Rio de Janeiro, Brazil, without cargo to return to Norfolk, Virginia. Several weeks later it was seen by the crew of a **lightship**. The schooner was under full sail with the crew all on deck. One of the crew shouted that they had lost both anchors. Two days later the ship was found beached on the shore with the sails still set and the lifeboats and crew's belongings on board. The crew was missing and was never seen again.

Marine Sulphur Queen

The *Marine Sulphur Queen,* a cargo ship, vanished in 1963. It left Texas carrying a cargo of molten sulphur. A search began when the ship could not be contacted after it failed to send a routine radio message. Some remains, including a foghorn and a life jacket, were found.

The *Mary Celeste*

Easily the most famous mystery of the sea is the case of the Mary Celeste, *a small sail-powered cargo ship. It was found drifting without its crew in 1872.*
The case of the Mary Celeste *is often linked with the Bermuda Triangle, but it was actually found near the Azores, which are closer to Spain than America. According to many accounts of the case, the ship appeared normal. All the crew's possessions and all the cargo were on board. It seemed that the crew had magically vanished. However, the rigging was damaged, the lifeboat was missing, and the hold was full of sea water. The most likely explanation is that the crew was convinced that the ship was about to sink, and they hurriedly abandoned it without taking down the sails. The ship continued to sail, leaving them behind in mid-ocean in an overloaded lifeboat.*

Into Thin Air

In all these following cases of aircraft that have disappeared in the Bermuda Triangle, not a scrap of the aircraft or any sign of survivors was ever found.

Flight 19

The case of Flight 19 is the most famous of all. It is mysterious because a group of five U.S. Navy bombers vanished at the same time, along with the search plane that was sent to find them. This seems like a very unlikely event. There are many different accounts of this case, but here are the basic facts.

This Martin Mariner seaplane is similar to the one that was sent to search for Flight 19.

At 2:00 P.M. on December 5, 1945, five Avenger Torpedo Bombers took off in good weather from Fort Lauderdale, Florida, on a routine training mission. It should have lasted two hours. The first signs of trouble appeared at 3:45 P.M., when the pilots realized they were lost. The flight leader, Lieutenant Taylor, reported that both his compasses were not working. A flight instructor from the Fort Lauderdale base offered to fly south to meet them, but Taylor replied, "I know where I am now. Don't come after me."

When voice communication stopped at 4:25 P.M., a Martin Mariner seaplane was sent to search for them. The last, faint radio signal, just the letters FT (the call letters of Flight 19), was received at the base about 7:00 P.M. Nothing more was heard from any of the Avengers or the rescue seaplane. An air–sea rescue search continued for weeks, but they found no sign of the 27 airmen or their aircraft.

Star Tiger

After flying from the Azores, the British airliner *Star Tiger*, a Tudor IV airliner, vanished in 1948. It had nearly reached Bermuda when the pilot radioed that the weather was good and that he expected to arrive on time. But the aircraft never arrived. A search for survivors and wreckage found nothing.

Douglas DC-3

This airliner vanished in 1948. It was flying to Miami, Florida, from Puerto Rico. The pilot reported by radio that he was 50 miles (80 kilometers) south of the airfield. But soon after this, the airfield could not get a response from the DC-3. A search found no sign of the aircraft, even though the water in the area where it disappeared was only 20 feet (6 meters) deep. The DC-3 had simply vanished.

This Avro Tudor airliner is similar to the Star Tiger *that disappeared in 1948.*

Did You See That?

Many people have had strange experiences in the Bermuda Triangle, but lived to tell the tale. Here are their stories.

Crew of Boeing 707

Soon after takeoff from San Juan, Puerto Rico, in 1963, the crew of a Boeing 707 saw the sea below them froth up for about 30 seconds. The disturbed area was about half a mile (one kilometer) across. The froth reached over two thousand feet (several hundred meters) into the air.

Chuck Wakely

In 1964, Chuck Wakely was flying from Nassau in the Bahamas to Miami, Florida. He noticed a faint glow on the wings of his aircraft, which gradually increased to a blinding light. At the same time, the aircraft's electrical equipment began to fail. After five minutes, the glow gradually faded and things returned to normal.

Captain Don Henry

Don Henry, captain of a **salvage tug**, was towing a barge in 1966 when the tug experienced electrical and engine failures. The compass started spinning out-of-control. When Henry went on deck, he found that the horizon was obscured by fog, the sea was choppy, and the barge was invisible, but the tow rope was still tight. After a while the engines began working again, and the tug moved forward. The barge reappeared, but it felt warm to the touch.

Bruce Gernon

In 1970, Bruce Gernon was flying a small private aircraft through the Bermuda Triangle when he flew into a "strange cloud." His instruments and compass failed while he was in the cloud, and he felt weightless for a few seconds. When he landed, he realized that his flight had taken half an hour less than he thought was possible for the flight.

Crew of the USS *Richard E. Byrd*

In 1971, the naval destroyer USS *Richard E. Byrd* lost the use of all its communications equipment on its voyage to Bermuda. The ship was lost and helpless at sea for more than a week before its radio began to work again.

Crew of the *Hollyhock*

In 1974, the **radar** aboard the *Hollyhock*, a U.S. Coast Guard boat, detected a large land mass in the ocean. The radar was checked and seemed to be working properly. Other ships also reported the same event. As the boat traveled towards the land mass, the "phantom island" disappeared.

*Many stories of strange happenings in the Bermuda Triangle involve **navigational** instruments. Could this be the key to solving the mystery?*

The Theories

What are the possible explanations for the strange cases reported on the previous pages? A look at marine and air accidents all over the world shows that there is a wide range of explanations for every Bermuda Triangle event.

If the number of accidents and disappearances in the Bermuda Triangle is compared to the number of ships and aircraft passing through it, the Bermuda Triangle does not seem to be a particularly dangerous place. In fact, Lloyd's, the world's shipping insurer, says that there are no more losses in the Bermuda Triangle than in any other shipping area.

A simple explanation

Most losses at sea and in the air are not in the slightest bit mysterious—and that includes losses in the Bermuda Triangle. Losses are caused by mechanical failure, bad weather, human error, or a combination of all three.

There are several ways a ship can sink. A ship's **hull** can be holed by hitting an object in or under the water, which allows water in from underneath. A ship can be damaged in a collision. A ship can simply break apart. A ship can capsize because it is top heavy, overloaded, or its cargo moves to one side. Obviously, bad weather makes all these events more likely. In the case of a collision, a smaller craft might be hit and sunk by a much larger craft without the crew of the larger craft even noticing, especially at night.

A **structural failure** in an aircraft, such as the loss of a wing, or a control failure, such as the **rudder** jamming, can bring an aircraft down very quickly. Dangerous cargo or leaking fuel tanks in ships and aircraft can cause fires or explosions.

Human factors

Mistakes by ships' crews and aircraft pilots can cause accidents. At sea, where there are no landmarks, **navigational** errors can lead to ships and aircraft becoming hopelessly lost. This is almost certainly what happened to the ill-fated Flight 19—the aircraft probably ran out of fuel and crashed into the ocean. Poor design or poor maintenance can also be responsible for mechanical failures. A few ships also disappear without a trace because of **insurance** fraud, **sabotage,** or the actions of modern-day pirates.

This old DC-3 airliner is on landing approach. In the 1940s, aircraft did not have the sophisticated navigation equipment that today's aircraft have.

Strange Weather

The seas in the Bermuda Triangle are often featured in vacation brochures. They look calm, turquoise, and shallow. But in fact, the area can have very bad storms. Storms can range from brief thunderstorms to tornadoes and **hurricanes**. The storms are often more sudden and violent than anywhere else in the world. Does the weather hold the answer to some of the mysterious disappearances?

Hurricanes and storms

Hurricanes are enormous, swirling storms. They begin in the Atlantic Ocean near the equator and move north, usually into the Caribbean Sea and the Gulf of Mexico. Winds in the center of a hurricane can reach speeds of more than 93 miles (150 kilometers) per hour. Wind gusts can reach speeds of 186 miles (300 kilometers) per hour.

Thunderstorms can be huge and severe in the Bermuda Triangle. They are created when warm, damp air rises into the atmosphere and **condenses**. Clouds can reach as high as 50,000 feet (15,000 meters) and measure several miles (or kilometers) across. Under the clouds are strong, gusty winds. Sometimes there are small, hurricane-like mini-storms.

This hurricane was photographed from space. The strongest winds are near the center of the cloud swirl.

16

These super strong hurricane and storm winds and the huge waves they create can overwhelm and capsize small boats. The winds can blow them off course. The waves can cause ships to break apart. Inside the storm clouds, the winds are very turbulent—they blow up and down as well as sideways. Aircraft flying through these clouds are tossed about. Occasionally they are tossed so fiercely that the airplane is damaged.

A waterspout is a tornado that sucks up water from the sea. It destroys any small craft in its way.

Freak waves

Even large ships have been capsized by individual **freak waves**. These waves can be up to 115 feet (35 meters) high. The freak waves may be caused by undersea earthquakes, volcanic eruptions, landslides on the **continental shelf,** or storm waves building together.

Currents

The water in the Bermuda Triangle also has strong **currents** flowing in it. These include the strong, north-flowing current called the Gulf Stream, which flows at about four miles (seven kilometers) per hour. Wind blowing in the opposite direction to the current can create very steep waves, which can swamp and capsize small craft. These currents could explain the unsuccessful air–sea searches in the Bermuda Triangle. By the time the rescue services arrived at the scene of the accident, the wreckage would have been swept away.

Electricity and Magnetism

Many travelers in the Bermuda Triangle experience strange magnetic and electrical effects, such as spinning compasses, failed electrical equipment, drained batteries, radio interference, and unusual lights. Can natural **phenomena** explain these effects?

Lightning

The heat created by a lightning strike can cause explosions on ships and in aircraft. Sparks can ignite fuel or fuel vapor inside empty fuel tanks. The explosions can sink wooden ships by punching holes in the hull. Huge **electric currents** in lightning also create strong **magnetic fields** that can cause compasses and radio communications to fail.

Lightning happens when static electricity builds up inside a cloud and then jumps to the ground.

Ball lightning

Ball lightning is very rare and not fully understood by scientists. This type of lightning could explain some of the strange lights seen in the Bermuda Triangle. It comes in the form of a ball of colored light about 10 inches (25 centimeters) across. It forms in **electrical storms**. The ball can hover and move about, as if under remote control.

18

Strange magnetic fields

The earth acts as a giant magnet. Its **magnetic poles** are near, but not in the same place as, its **geographic poles**. A magnetic compass points toward magnetic north, which is the direction toward the magnetic North Pole. In most places on the earth's surface, there is a difference between magnetic north and true north. But the Bermuda Triangle is on a line through both the geographic North Pole and the magnetic North Pole. The two directions are the same. A compass pointing to true north seems strange to sailors and pilots from other areas of the world. This could explain some **navigational** errors in the Bermuda Triangle.

Another confusing compass error, which happens in many areas of the world, including some parts of the Bermuda Triangle, is when the compass turns away from magnetic north. These incidents are often caused by underground deposits of iron ore or magnetic rocks. They distort the earth's magnetic field. The effect is called a **magnetic anomaly**. Temporary magnetic anomalies could also be caused by **magma** flowing near the earth's surface, undersea earthquakes, or electrical storms. It is possible that these events could set up very strong magnetic fields that could affect electrical equipment as well as compasses.

A piece of iron changes the shape of a magnet's field, just as magnetic rocks affect the earth's magnetic field.

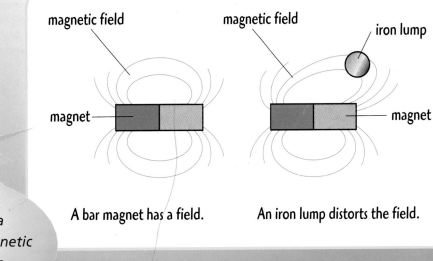

magnetic field

magnet

A bar magnet has a field.

magnetic field

iron lump

magnet

An iron lump distorts the field.

Weird and Wonderful

Several books about the Bermuda Triangle claim that the strange events that happen there cannot have natural explanations. These authors ask, "How can huge ships and whole groups of aircraft simply disappear in calm weather and shallow seas?" They say that because there is no evidence, supernatural forces must be involved.

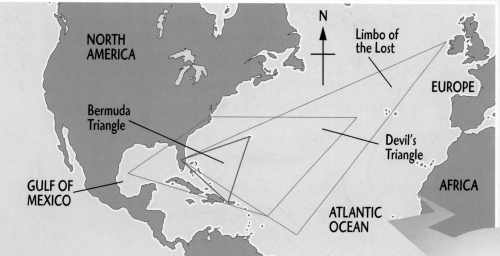

Writers who dispute the boundaries of the Bermuda Triangle are able to include more disappearances in their arguments.

Vile vortices

Ivan T. Sanderson drew a map of twelve areas where strange disappearances happen. He included the Bermuda Triangle in his map. He calls these areas "vile **vortices**," where there are massive **magnetic anomalies** that create "time-slips." He says these time slips mysteriously transport objects to other places on Earth. However, there seems to be no statistical evidence to support his ideas.

Aliens and Atlantis

One of the most popular theories for disappearances in the Bermuda Triangle is alien abduction. Some people believe that the ships and aircraft, or the people on them, have been carried away by aliens for investigation and experimentation. Ivan T. Sanderson claims that the ships and aircraft could have been taken to an advanced civilization under the ocean below the Bermuda Triangle.

Underwater ruins near the island of Bimini are claimed to be the remains of Atlantis.

Charles Berlitz is the most famous Bermuda Triangle writer. He has suggested that Atlantis, the legendary lost land, was on the western edge of the Bermuda Triangle near the island of Bimini. He says that Atlantis's technology is still there, sinking ships and shooting down aircraft. The legend of Atlantis comes from writings of the Greek philosopher Plato. There is no proof that it ever existed.

Black holes

Vincent Gaddis, the man who first used the phrase "Bermuda Triangle" in 1964, suggested that ships and planes may disappear through a gateway. He says this gateway is possibly like a mini **black hole** that takes ships and aircraft into another time or universe. This could explain why some aircraft traveling through the Bermuda Triangle arrive at their destination more quickly than should have been possible. However, **navigational** errors and unexpected strong winds are more likely explanations.

A Modern Theory

In 1995, an international organization called the Ocean Drilling Program began looking for new energy sources. They were looking for **methane** on the ocean floor between Bermuda and the eastern coast of the United States. Methane is a gas. It is created when dead animals and plants **decompose** in the **sediments** on the ocean floor. This gas might be escaping from the rocks under the ocean floor and could possibly be used as energy. What does this have to do with the Bermuda Triangle? Perhaps huge bubbles of methane, rising to the surface, affect the ships and aircraft above.

Gas hydrates

The strange thing about the methane that the drillers found was that it was in the form of gas hydrate. This means that it was mixed with frozen water. In methane hydrate, the methane is trapped inside the ice. Methane hydrate forms when a mixture of water and methane is squeezed by very high pressure deep under the sea bed. When the pressure is released or the temperature rises, the methane is released. When just one quart (about one liter) of icy hydrate melts, it releases 45 gallons (170 liters) of methane.

Methane released from the ocean floor could explain some accidents on oil and gas drilling rigs.

Scientists think there is a huge amount of methane hydrate under the oceans, including under the Bermuda Triangle.

Bubble trouble

Imagine what would happen if a deposit of methane hydrate under the ocean floor was released into the water. This could happen during massive underwater landslides or earthquakes. Remember that a small amount of hydrate makes a huge amount of gas. The bubble of gas would rush toward the surface, expanding as it rose.

If a huge bubble rose under a ship, it would produce a massive hole in the sea underneath it. The ship would drop into the hole, sink instantly, settle to the sea bed, and be covered in sediment disturbed by the escaping gas.

The methane gas might also cause problems for aircraft above the water. Methane is lighter than air, so it would rise upwards after leaving the water. An aircraft flying through this area might suffer engine failure or it might ignite the gas bubble. There is also evidence that a huge rush of gas would create a strong **magnetic field** that would affect compasses.

This diagram shows what could happen to a ship if a huge bubble rose underneath it.

Melting gas hydrate causes a methane bubble on the sea bed.

The bubble rises to the surface.

The ship above falls into the "hole" caused by the bubble.

The ship fills with water and sinks.

True or False?

There are no reports of disappearances being faked in the Bermuda Triangle, but there are many cases of the truth about disappearances being ignored. Most of the books about the Bermuda Triangle discuss cases of ships and aircraft that have disappeared or been abandoned. But sometimes the facts of the cases are misquoted, misstated, or simply ignored in order to create a mystery. Here are some of the cases.

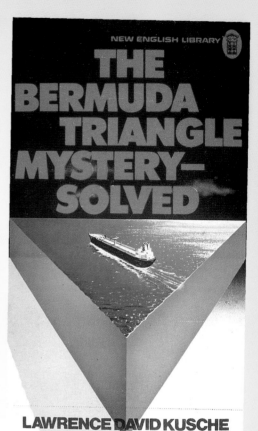

NEW ENGLISH LIBRARY

THE BERMUDA TRIANGLE MYSTERY— SOLVED

LAWRENCE DAVID KUSCHE

Flight 19

Five bombers and a rescue plane vanished in 1945. There are reports that the flight leader sent a message, "This is an emergency. We seem to be off course. We cannot see land . . . repeat . . . we cannot see land," and "We don't know which way is west. Everything is wrong . . . strange. We are not sure of any direction. The ocean doesn't look as it should." These reports are not true. The flight leader was very new to the area, and it's likely that he led the flight out to sea instead of back to land. Also, the Martin Mariner rescue plane did not simply disappear. A ship at sea saw an airplane explode at the same time the rescue plane disappeared from **radar** screens. The weather **deteriorated** badly, making the search almost impossible. Otherwise wreckage might have been found.

Lawrence David Kusche investigated the facts behind dozens of Bermuda Triangle "mysteries." He found that most had a simple answer.

Star Tiger

An airliner vanished in 1948.
Contrary to the stories of the captain reporting good flying conditions, the weather was not good. There were strong head winds and heavy cloud cover that made **navigation** difficult. The aircraft may also have run out of fuel because the strong head winds would have made the journey longer than expected.

DC-3

An airliner vanished in 1948.
There are false reports that the pilot said he could "see the lights of Miami." But it is likely that he was lost and over deep ocean. This DC-3 was known to have had a faulty radio, so it could not have made an emergency call.

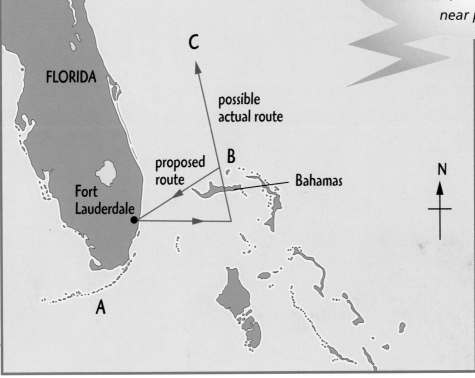

Lieutenant Taylor, leader of Flight 19, probably thought he was at point A when he was actually at point B. The planes flew north to reach land, but ran out of fuel near point C.

Muddled Reports

All of the following reports are of ships that, according to several writers, disappeared mysteriously in the Bermuda Triangle. Again, there is more to the stories than is often reported.

Atalanta

The *Atalanta* was a training ship that disappeared in 1880. It was on a voyage that included sailing through the Bermuda Triangle. What the reports do not mention is that no one knows where the ship actually vanished. It also had a very inexperienced crew and would have encountered bad weather in the area where it was sailing.

Rubicon

In October 1944, this 90-ton Cuban cargo ship was found drifting and abandoned off Florida. Only a dog was on board. The crew had mysteriously vanished. Or had they? Reports from the time say the *Rubicon* was in port in Havana, Cuba, when the **moorings** broke in a **hurricane**. The ship drifted away, leaving the crew stranded ashore.

Bella

This British ship was sailing from Rio de Janeiro, Brazil, to Jamaica in 1854 when it vanished "without a trace." The *Bella* was probably overloaded and may have capsized. Wreckage was found six days after it left Rio, when it would have been nowhere near the Bermuda Triangle.

Freya

The German **bark** *Freya* was found with its crew gone and its masts broken after sailing from Cuba. Supposedly a victim of the Bermuda Triangle, it was, in fact, sailing from Mexico and found in the Pacific Ocean, not the Atlantic.

Raifuku Maru

This Japanese freighter vanished in the Bermuda Triangle in 1925. Before disappearing, it sent the alarming radio message, "Danger like dagger now. Come quick!" This message may be made up, since there was radio interference. The passenger liner *Homeric* actually saw the *Raifuku Maru* sink in huge waves with all the crew aboard.

Charles Berlitz's bestselling book tells of "unexplained" mysteries.

Why falsify stories?

People are more interested in the mysterious than the **mundane**. Books about mysterious events are often bestsellers. This is certainly true of the Bermuda Triangle mystery. Several writers have written books that build up this mystery by telling only half the story.

The most famous of Bermuda Triangle authors is Charles Berlitz, who wrote two books in the 1970s. The first, *The Bermuda Triangle*, sold 20 million copies in 30 languages and made Berlitz a wealthy man. His books led to television programs, newspaper articles, and more books about what actually may not be a mystery at all.

CHARLES BERLITZ

the bermuda triangle

Panther Illustrated 586 04272 5

The bestselling saga of unexplained disappearances

In Conclusion

Of all the world's mysteries, that of the Bermuda Triangle seems to be the one supported by the weakest evidence. On one side of the argument are writers who claim supernatural explanations. They ignore scientific evidence of violent storms, **magnetic anomalies,** and strong **currents**. On the other side of the argument are people, including scientists, who claim that there is no mystery at all. They say the disappearances have natural causes and are no more frequent than probability would suggest. This side includes the United States government, the U. S. Coast Guard, and the U. S. Navy.

This picture postcard view of the Bermuda coast has nothing strange in sight!

There is no doubt that there are a few truly mysterious cases. Sometimes a ship, boat, or plane was definitely inside the Bermuda Triangle and really did disappear without a trace.

But when so many of the "mysterious" disappearances of ships, aircraft, and people actually have believable, natural explanations, the biggest mystery is how the Bermuda Triangle mystery ever started!

Make up your own mind

Now that you have read about the Bermuda Triangle and the possible explanations for the disappearances there, what are your conclusions? Are there theories you can dismiss without further investigation? Do you have any theories of your own?

What about the supernatural theory or the time-slip theory? Can you rule them out? Perhaps one is the answer, but it depends on scientific principles that we don't understand. While it might be strange that no trace of a ship or an aircraft is found, can this be taken as proof that something mysterious is going on? Do you think that bad weather and human error are more likely explanations? And what about the **methane** hydrate theory? Could this be the answer?

Try to keep an open mind. Remember, if scientists throughout history had not investigated everything that appeared strange or mysterious, many scientific discoveries may never have been made.

Mysteries make good reading. This article from the People *newspaper in 1991 simply retells tales from the Bermuda Triangle.*

Fateful flight of the Avengers

AIRMEN VANISH WITHOUT TRACE

EVER since the first seamen set sail, the vast oceans have been sources of myth and mystery.

Best documented of these was last century's riddle of the Mary Celeste, the ship which was found eerily abandoned in the Atlantic, east of the Azores.

Her sails were tattered and below deck there was chilling evidence which suggested hurried flight – yet the ship's log remained intact and its last entry, made nine days before, gave no hint of impending trouble.

The mystery remained unsolved even after a British Vice Admiralty court of inquiry, as it does today.

Far more recently, voyagers of the sea and of the air have come to fear the Bermuda Triangle, a vaguely defined area somewhere east of Bermuda.

One student of the unexplained, Ivan Sanderson, has theorised that the mysterious triangle is one of a dozen areas called "vile vortices" – another infamous vortex is the so-called Devil's Sea off the coast of Japan – where baffling forces are said to cause ships to vanish.

One of the earliest of these fateful missions in the Bermuda Triangle began on December 5, 1945, when five US Avenger torpedo bombers

roared off the runway of the Fort Lauderdale Naval Air Station in Florida.

Flight Instructor Lieutenant Charles G Taylor was leading 13 crewmen of Flight 19 on a routine navigational training exercise. Their course lay over an area bounded by Bermuda, Florida and Puerto Rico – the area which is now recognised as the Bermuda Triangle.

Flight 19 began smoothly enough but at 3.40pm an unsettling message from Taylor to another plane in the squadron was picked up by Lieutenant Robert Cox who was at that moment airborne over Fort Lauderdale on another exercise.

"What is your trouble?" Cox asked Taylor.

"Both my compasses are out and I am trying to find Fort Lauderdale," Taylor replied.

For 45 minutes Cox tried to ascertain Taylor's position and to direct him to land by orienting him towards the sun. But although it was a clear day, Taylor seemed unable to find it.

Finally, Taylor's transmission faded until it stopped. Then, inexplic... radio went dead, too, and he returned to the field at Fort Lauderdale. The ground station at Port Everglades...

ever, had established intermittent contact with the troubled Flight 19, confirming Cox's observations. Finally, at about 5.15pm the ground station heard a forlorn message from Flight 19:

"We'll fly west until we hit the beach or run out of gas."

The authorities at Fort Lauderdale ordered a search but the Mariner was not heard of again.

For the next five days, search planes flew more than 930 sorties over the area, but not a scrap of wreckage from either the Avengers or the Mariner was ever recovered.

Most analysts blame these and other disappearances in the area on normal hazards of the sea and air. But what happened still remains a profound mystery.

More recently, we have learned of an equally mysterious leap across space and time, which occurred within the triangle – 25 years after the flight of the Avengers, almost to the day.

There was a "strange cigar-shaped cloud," recalled Bruce Gernon Jr, which gave him the first hint that his flight on December 4, 1970, would be...

Gernon had just taken off in his Beachcraft Bonanza from Andros Island in the Bahamas, bound for Palm Beach, Florida.

He remembers accelerating quickly to avoid the thick cloud, but it seemed to rise to meet him.

The plane seemed to pick up unnatural speed, and for several seconds Gernon and his father experienced weightlessness. Then the aeroplane entered a greenish-white haze – not the blue sky he had seen ahead.

Through the haze he spotted a stretch of land and, calculating his flight time, took it to be the Bimini Keys, an island east of Miami. Minutes later, Gernon recognised it as Miami beach itself.

Landing at Palm Beach, Gernon checked his clock. A trip that normally took him about 75 minutes had taken him only 45. And he had burned 12 fewer gallons of fuel than usual.

To this day, Gernon considers himself a lucky voyager in the Bermuda Triangle, having lived to tell of the inexplicable time warp...

29

Glossary

bark type of sailing cargo ship with three masts, popular in the late 19th century

black hole region of space where gravity is so strong that not even light can escape from it

collier medium-sized cargo ship designed to carry bulk cargoes, such as coal

condense turn from gas to liquid because of cooling

continental shelf edge of a continent, where the depth of the ocean increases dramatically

current flow of water in a certain direction

decompose to break down complex chemicals into more simple chemicals, occurring in animals and plants when they die

deteriorate to get worse

electrical storm storm in which there is lightning and thunder

electric current flow of an electrical charge from one place to another

freak wave wave considerably larger than normal waves on the water, caused by smaller waves building up together

geographic pole one of the two points (North Geographic Pole and South Geographic Pole) where the axis around which the earth revolves meets the earth's surface

hull main part of a boat or ship, forming its structure and keeping the craft watertight

hurricane intense weather system that creates torrential rain and winds of more than 90 miles (150 kilometers) per hour (called cyclones in the southern hemisphere)

insurance money paid to a person when his or her property is damaged, lost, or stolen

lightship permanently anchored ship with a beacon to guide other ships

magma hot, molten rock underground

magnetic anomaly place on the earth's surface where the earth's magnetic field is distorted

magnetic field area around a magnet where its magnetic force is felt

magnetic pole one of the two places on the earth (called the North Magnetic Pole and the South Magnetic Pole) where the earth's magnetic field is strongest

methane naturally occurring gas often found under the ground with oil

mooring place or object to which boats are tied

mundane ordinary, commonplace

navigational to do with navigation—the planning and following of a route at sea or in the air

phenomenon remarkable or unexplained happening

plankton mass of tiny animals and plants that live in a body of water

radar device used to locate objects and determine their size and the speed at which they are moving

rudder device at the stern (rear) that is used to turn a boat, ship, or aircraft from side to side

sabotage to deliberately make things go wrong

salvage tug large tug used for towing ships or oil rigs, or for recovering ships after accidents

schooner traditional type of sailing ship with two or more masts

sediment mud, silt, sand, or small pieces of rock that settles on the bottom of a liquid

sloop small sailing ship

structural failure failure of the actual structure of a ship or plane, such as a hull breaking into two pieces or a wing snapping off

vortex (plural **vortices**) fast-spinning swirl of air or water

More Books to Read

Abels, Harriette S. *Bermuda Triangle.* Parsippany, N.J.: Silver Burdett Press, 1987.

Collins, Jim. *The Bermuda Triangle.* Austin, Tex.: Raintree Steck-Vaughn, 1983.

Innes, Brian. *The Bermuda Triangle.* Austin, Tex.: Raintree Steck-Vaughn, 1999.

Index